Life As A Depressed Person

By: Kathy Lenz Toavs

To order additional copies of this book, contact:
Xlibris Corporation
1-888-795-4274
www.Xlibris.com
Orders@Xlibris.com

Preface

This is my story about my life of living with depression for the last ten years. I am not in the medical profession, but I am a sufferer of this dreaded illness. I hope my experiences will help a few people come to terms with their lives.

No one understands unless they have been there and frustration runs high with everyone including our caregivers and families.

Dedicated to my friend Linda who was very open with her illness and to those suffering depression may you have inner peace.

Chapter 1:

Why

I won't go into my life history as so many people have the same type of family lives. One of my cousins recently remarked that she came from a dysfunctional family. My response was, there is not a functional family alive. My reasoning we all have problems with either loving, communication, family placement or the question "am I genetically prone to this illness. And on and on. To find blame does not solve any problems we may face in life. I feel as though I am a spiritual person and that we handle our problems with the strength we have. Maybe the big guy up there rolls the dice and the numbers come up one way or the other. Who knows? Not I!

As we march through this life encounters of all kind come our way some interesting and some challenging. I believe how we deal with them is essential to our life hereafter. Don't think I at take depression lightly. Many times I have lain in bed and prayed for God to take me. The ad on T.V. with the lady being cranked up as she tries to get through the day is so appripoe of how I feel. Who would have thought; there I go. Please God, give me strength to deal with my problems.

Chapter: 2

Doctors

I have been under the assumption that certain traumas in life such as death, divorce, children leaving the nest, etc. are the key to bringing depression on.

One of my doctors asked me some interesting questions. One of the questions was if you wake up in the morning with your mind racing? My response was "I have ever since I was a child." That was the clue that this horrible illness has been habitating in my mind and body for years. I have had some very good doctors. Remember you know your body and if you don't feel right with medication be sure and let your medical professional know.

This past winter I was on a certain medication that was not good for me. Actually I was there physically, but not mentally. Finally one day I confided in my husband that I was going to stop the medication. [Don't take my advice — remember I am not medically certified.] I went through several months of horrendous withdrawals and anxiety. I am sure that I would not do that again, but I am thankful I am off that medication. I did have anxiety medication and made it through, but with several interesting incidents along the way. We were traveling and living in our fifth wheel last winter. One morning my husband was out walking the dog. I heated a rice bag up in the microwave to set against my back in the mornings, to help me relax. The breaker box kept flipping. My husband had placed the garbage sack the night before in front of the breaker box so he would remember to take it out the next day. The garbage was still sitting there when I awoke. After several tries to warm the rice bag, the breaker kept flipping, so I, in my anger, opened the door and threw it out with gusto. Needless to say the garbage sack made a large crash when it landed.

Later when my husband opened the door he placed the dog in the fifth wheel, turned around, grabbed the sack and proceeded to the garbage located passed the other R.V.'s. A man I called Budweizer Bob was two doors down. He remarked that my husband had a beeper on his butt too. He had made the same comment about some other gentleman in the park a few days before (meaning the wife has control). Well, my husband came back and told me what he had said! I was so ashamed.

Right next to us lived a couple I called "the Christians." They were such a nice couple. They kept to themselves, visiting only when the right chance presented itself. I thought, what if they heard that? Before we left I went over and apologized to them and Ron said he had not heard anything. He remarked, "you have anger issues." My response was "I have had anger issues since I was young." That got me thinking "yes I do." I explained that I had gone off my medication But really that was no excuse. He then proceeded to tell me about his depression. It seems people want to share if they know someone else has depression. I think they have hope there will be some solution that can be shared.

One time when I was nine I was upset with my mother and I broke a table knife in half with my hands as I sat at the table. It hurt only me as the silver ware set was a gift from my Godmother, whom I adored. Lesson learned, control my temper. Mother didn't say a word. She was a very wise woman.

Chapter 3:

Shame

Do not let depression make you feel ashamed and stop you from living your life. This illness can manifest itself in anyone. I may not have sought medical help but a friend had shared with me her struggle with the illness. Through her openess she helped me and I know she has helped many other people. "God Bless Her." Not everyone is secure enough to share their private lives in such a way.

Pacing became a habit of mine at first, as I thought I could walk it away. My youngest son said "Mom you should join the Olympics," as he watched me pacing outside. One day after my pacing and ringing my hands I went back into the house and found my husband sitting in his chair with his head in his hands crying. I was so shocked — then I realized the effect it was having on my whole family.

I asked my husband to take me to the hospital immediately. In the hospital they took me to a room to ask what was wrong and I just gripped sink and begged them to help me. The doctor came in and talked to me so patiently and sincerely. They gave me an anxiety relaxant and then he recommended I go to a doctor trained in mental health. I was given the name of a good doctor and made an appointment as soon as I could see the doctor. That started my journey with the medical profession.

I have had three different doctors and now seem to have found a doctor that is on the right wavelength with my illness.

I have tried several prescriptions over the years and some seemed to work but several I couldn't tolerate. It seems to me after a while I would become immune to the medication. I use to be very active, but have slowed down due to this illness. I need exercise and have to push myself now to get it. My beautiful yard was my passion after my boys grew up and left home. I became overwhelmed with it when I became sick. My husband had to take over as I could not get myself to even mow the lawn. Even walking around the yard did not interest me and I use to get so much strength just walking through my beautiful trees. The energy around them is amazing.

A meditation garden I had started few years ago but have yet to finish it. I planned to fill it with flowers, trees, shrubs and my love. Also being a water lover also, I have plans for a pond for solitude.

When I can just get one project a day finished such as dusting or cleaning the mirrors, it makes me feel so much better. It is such a chore to get started. This is the woman that decided one summer to paint all the corrals and cattle shed. A very large undertaking. I did it all and ended up with tennis elbow for several months from overwork! I remember being frustrated that I could not work like I had been all summer.

Chapter 4:

Recluse

Shying away from people is one way to protect ourselves. Depression makes us go deeper and deeper into our shells. We seem to be leary of crowds and even people on a one-on-one basis. Too bad as we need to be around people. Why when there is no enjoyment to life. Smile and acting like we are having a good time is something we become good at. Forcing ourselves it is nearly impossible to socialize. If something is planned that we are to attend we can work ourselves into a frenzy just worrying about the coming event.

My best friend and I hadn't seen each other in two years until recently. Since we were in grade school together we have had a friendship. We had such a nice time when we did get together.

Then there are the friends you scare away because they do not understand your illness. They are fearful that you will take them down to where you are.

Chapter 5:

Sunlight

Being a reader I started to research Seasonal Depression (SAD) after a discussion with my doctor. I did some reading and learned so much about my life. Yes, I did need the Sun in fact, my body yearned for it. Reading whatever I could get my hands on, I found full spectrum lights that recreate sunlight as close as possible. A sun box is also very good but they are a bit expensive. I know a person that uses the sunbox faithfully. Also vitamin D is given off by the sun. We now use full spectrum lights wherever possible in our home and fifth wheel.

Looking back at my youth I remember my mother always had the rooms we were occupying full of light. She would always leave lights on so when we came home at night we would enter a house full of light. I, being conservative, always turn most lights off when not in certain rooms. Not good for a positive outlook on life. Always trying to save money it is still hard for me to leave lights on. I do seek out the sunlight, even just sitting by a window the sun shines through.

I have observed people and they seem much happier when the sun is shining. We are drawn to sunshine. The Northwest U.S. seems to have a higher number of depression cases than the rest of the U.S. They don't have much sun light in the winter and lots of rainy, dreary days. I understand the feeling.

Having helped in the schools years ago I had a friend who was a full time secretary was having some problems. I knew her quite well and we had lengthy discussions several times I told her having extra full spectrum lights would help if she could get the janitor to install them, I would give her a few for the office. A month or so later she approached me and told me what a difference they had made for her.

One worry I have with our schools is most classrooms do not have many windows. I understand the children look out the windows and having fewer windows is a deterent for gawkers. My belief, though, is we would have more productive students and teachers if we had the proper light for them. People are drawn to the sun. It heals our minds, souls, bodies and gives us a positive outlook for our lives I believe.

Think about how our universe is designed. God created such a wonderment. My feeling is we have no clue as to our wonderful creation, and definitely do not appreciate our natural habitat. Walk by trees, stand still and close your eyes until you can feel their wonderful energy. My husband has read that animals will go to pine trees and lay underneath for peace, safety and protection. Stand, walk, or sit on the ground or a bench. Wear moccasins, or better yet be barefoot, and feel the grass or the soil on your feet. Sit on Mother Earth and grab a handfull of her life (soil). Let it heal you.

If you have a pet, it is good to hold them on your lap as they are so soothing for our nerves. Just rest your hand on them or pet them. My husband usually has his small dog on his lap when he is sitting in the house and it calms him very much. People who ride horses for pleasure seem to be much happier, especially if they have a special horse. When we were first married we had horses and I loved to pet them or just watch them. Animals have a special instinct, a connection with nature.

My mother-in-law would always tell me to go outside in the mornings and breathe the fresh air and be exposed to the sun for at least 15 minutes. That way you start the day right. Most of us need that cup of coffee in the morning. Drink your coffee (or whatever gets you going in the morning) by being outside or by a window that gives you full morning light. Give yourself that time. You deserve it. It won't be a cure all, but it will be a step in the right direction.

Chapter: 6

Exercise

This is one of the hardest things I have to encounter and I have heard so many of us just can't get those legs moving. Why bother when our mind does not care and it is near impossible to motivate ourselves.

A good friend of mine showed up at our home one morning when I was in the deep depths of my depression. I had not gotten out of bed yet and it was 10:30. She insisted she was not leaving unless I got out of the house and went for a drive. I used every excuse I could think of to put her off to no avail. I need to bathe I told her. Well, she said she would wait and yes, we did go for a nice long drive. I dreaded to go back home and yet my home has always been so special to me. I was really sick. I told her later she had saved my life as I was so deep into my depression.

This is hard for me to discuss, but it is a very serious problem. Depressed people need to go to the bathroom and have a good B.M. everyday if possible. I feel so much better. It is like a cleansing. The morning is good. If not, the day can drag on in more than one way. It seems that cleaning our system rids us of awful toxins that add to the misery of our illness. I wish I could recommend a good de-toxification program, but I do not know of one. Once again we know our own body and functions.

Vitamin supplement is one of my daily rituals. I have been a vitamin user my entire life and just feel most people could use some kind of supplement. Vitamins do not seem to have hurt me any and why take a chance as I am not one that always gets a balanced meal. I find there are days I don't feel like eating and then I hit the candy or sweets. Shame on me. One thing some anti depressants bring on is weight gain. So many of us have low self esteem because of our weight being to heavy or not thin enough. Our mental state is so fragile. If we have low self esteem we really do not like ourselves much and that adds to our depression.

Eating a good meal in a timely fashion is a good idea. It is so difficult when you do not feel like eating much less fixing a meal. We personally try to eat a lot of fish even though one of our sons is a cattleman. My husband is a meat eater and we do need the protein that comes from meat. Granted you can get protein from other sources.

Mother, when she was elderly would lift a soup can up and down to get exercise for her arms. We have a small set of dumbbells that I can use. I haven't been too faithful with any exercising it is so difficult to force myself sometimes. My oldest brother is adamant about getting exercise. He thinks if I can get enough exercise I will be ok. I always tell him he doesn't understand, but that is part of the sadness of depression. He feels I need mind over matter now. How do I control my mind when it is out of control? My brother is right, but does not really realize that once in awhile it is impossible. To tell yourself is one thing but to be able to do it is another. Our mind, so to speak, has a mind of its own.

Chapter 7

A lifetime

If you are taking anti depressants and feel good do not think automatically you are healed, as it usually is the medication helping your outlook on life. Tending to not want to take medication when you feel good is normal. We seem to think everything is ok now and we do not need the medication. Then we take three steps back and it is a struggle to re-coup where we were at. I have been told by my doctor that I may have to take anti depressants the rest of my life to which my husband is not happy. One step at a time is what I need to take and hopefully he will accept that. I think he likes me as a functioning human.

Alcohol and drugs do not mix and believe me I have felt the effects. When we were young we had a party hardy bunch of friends and it easily can become a habit. I enjoy my beer, especially when we barbeque. I love sitting on the deck enjoying the sunset and the socialization.

Anti depressant drugs and alcohol are a deadly mixture. "Think before you drink." We may think it makes us feel better, actually it just numbs us and the next day is horrible. "Been there done that".

Chapter 8:

"Laughter is the Best Medicine",

Laugh a good genuine laugh. It will do wonders for your spirit. I was at the dentist one day getting my teeth cleaned and the hygenist was visiting about some of her experiences a couple of winters ago when they went south. My husband and I were about to embark on our first sno-bird trip so I was having a good time listening. Some of the experiences she was reminiscing about were hilarious. Being a bit overweight, I laughed until my belly jiggled. What a wonderful experience, and this was at the dentist's office!

Recently my cousin and I were visiting about when we were kids. I laughed until I cried. It felt so good. We both enjoyed the evening so much. I have been doing so much better, and I do not know if it is from the new medication I am on, the laughter, or the fact that I am writing about my illness. It is so good to feel human again. I pray that it will last.

Chapter 9:

My Mother is Gone

My depression really kicked in after the death of my mother. I just went into a complete tailspin when the funeral was over and our family left. Mom was a very strong woman and she was very knowledgeable. My husband and I felt we could consult her about almost anything and she would give her honest opinion. Her encouragement and enthusiasm helped us so much. Without her there was a great void in our lives. I did not think I had the strength to go on without her. I have a very good marriage and my husband was so close to Mother it even effected him when she passed away

I basically closed down and ended whatever social life, work and relationships I had. I stayed at home and became a hermit. Why go out and smile when my heart felt like it was dead. At the drop of a hat I would cry. I became more sentimental than ever. I did not feel like eating, much less cooking. The pounds rolled off me and the only thing good was that I was slender. That was not the way to diet, believe me

I know Mother would be sad to know this is how I had been affected. I do not grieve for her, as with my faith, I believe she is at peace but it is grief for my loss of her. It is selfishness on my part to grieve so hard. Time does not numb us but does not take away the loneliness. My understanding is that major life changes can bring depression on. So be it—death brought on mine. I have been a sufferer of this illness for ten years and my husband and family still don't understand fully. My husband tries to be patient.

Chapter 10:

Suicide

Recently I read an obituary in the newspaper about a young man that had died. The family bravely stated he had commited suicide and that he had been suffering depression lately. I was so sad, but I was grateful for the honesty of his family. They had wanted him to seek help but he had not. I prayed for the young man and his family. They had given a gift to people who read this article. I hoped it would guide someone to seek help. So, through his suffering from depression and his death, the life of someone may be saved.

Some people get so desperate to get away from their depression they will do anything. That is when the end comes. To commit suicide is the ultimate act of escape. To become so desperate is sad, but it does happen to many. Life to them just is not worth living anymore.

Suicide, I know, is a fear for all caregivers. As in my case, my husband has hidden his pistol. When I have been really down, it has crossed my mind. We become so desperate and feel there is no solution to our own misery. My mind though has been clear enough to know I could not hurt my family with such an act. Thank you God for the strength you have given me to carry on with life.

Chapter 11:

The Caregiver

We get frustrated because the people close to us do not understand what we are going through. One morning when we were traveling I was having withdrawals from suddenly going off my medication. I had gone back to bed. My husband was upset and frustrated with me. I felt terrible and really wanted him close because I was actually afraid of how I felt. Hubby said he had to go to the R.V. office to check on something, so he was off. Later I could hear him outside visiting with the guys. After about two hours he returned and I was really hurt he had left me alone. I lashed out at him when he came back and I asked him if he had gotten his feelings soothed. My fear had overtaken me and he obviously did not know I was literally afraid of how I felt. He did not understand his feelings much less mine.

My husband could not understand why I did not do my everyday chores as usual. He would ask me if I had bathed. I used to love my bath and he wanted me to be soothed by soaking in the tub. Did you take your medicine? Caregivers want to make sure we do not forget or not want to take it.

Caregivers become our mothers in many ways, as though we are small children.

They protect us. They walk on eggshells for fear they will do or say the wrong thing. They want to see a glimmer of the person that we use to be. The caregivers draw back and get angry at others for not understanding what their loved one or themselves are going through.

My husband hoped to see a bit of the old me and would hang on my every word if I was having a good day. Seeing the person they love like this, caregivers themselves start to become depressed and draw back. Give space or stay away becomes a dilemma to our caregivers. Sometimes encouraging us to get out in the public or go for a walk works and sometimes it does not. Be forceful or not? Many times I have thanked my husband for getting me out and then there are the times I just refuse to budge. Just leave me alone!

Chapter 12:

Genetics

Looking back on my family, I see depression on my maternal side. There are at least three relatives who have suffered with depression. My Grandmother, an aunt and an uncle. I even feel my Mother had a bit of it as I referred to the lights in chapter five. This makes me think that depression is genetic.

In the past, the solution was to give shock treatments when the doctor considered a person really bad. Grandma and my aunt both had them. These treatments seemed to work, but they would lose their memory for a time. I saw personally what my grandmother went through when I was young and it was very sad for both her and I. Shock treatments were a severe solution to the problem. In those days there was a terrible stigma to anything to do with mental health. So much of it was hidden. The medicine we have now was not available to them. We have come a long way medically. I have been so desperate at times that I have asked my doctor if I could get shock treatments. I have not had them as the doctor was wise enough to discourage me.

Mother always said my grandmother needed to get her sleep. Grandma did not like to take anything to sleep. It made her feel groggy. That is one reason she had such trouble with depression, she didn't get her sleep and that in itself, made her sick. Lack of sleep intensified her illness.

In my opinion this illness seems to manifest itself in people that have a high expectation of themselves. Our minds race all the time and usually with things that we just can not put to rest.

Chapter 13:

Sleep

We yearn for sleep. To be out of our life and into our dreams. Sometimes dreams are much better than reality. We awake and try to go back to sleep again and again. The escape is what we want, as our life is so miserable in our mind.

Then we go through stages when we wake up at every hour in the night, not able to go back to sleep. I now get up every morning at four or five o'clock. I am writing now, so it is okay. When I am not in the mood to write or have no projects, believe me, four in the morning can be too early.

Sleep can become such a problem. Our bodies need to be tired to get restful sleep and if we are not physical during the day our bodies are not tired. Yet we force ourselves to sleep, and then we don't get the solid good rest we really need. This magnifies our illness to the point we are our own worst enemy, both physically and mentally. Sometimes I need sleep so bad I will sleep all day and night, and then the next day I feel like I am human. This is a gift I give myself. When a person gets broken sleep during the night it is worse than not having gotten any sleep.

I have spent many days not even getting dressed and it does not seem to bother me one bit. Years ago I would have been so ashamed to even think of not getting dressed for the day.

To spend the day in and out of bed just to get through the day. To wait for night to come so we can go back to bed for the night hoping when we wake the next day we will feel better.

Chapter 14:

Our Destiny?

Living the life of a depressed person, I do not know if one day is going to be good or will I be as they say "bummed out." Life is a roller coaster for me and it is impossible to plan anything, as I do not know how I will feel. If something is planned I can work myself into a frenzy just worrying about the coming occasion.

Struggling with this illness effects me in so many different ways. I need to remember that people are a unique gift from God to the world. There must be a message I can receive that will help me with my life. It is not overnite that I will receive help, but I need to keep trying to keep a positive attitude and have hope that one day I will be well again. I believe it is possible with some help and my own strength .